DO
as I Do,
Not as I Did

Helpful Tips to Starting a Successful Business

J. L. SPRATLING

DO
as I Do,
Not as I Did

Helpful Tips to Starting a Successful Business

Do as I Do, Not as I Did: Helpful Tips to Starting a Successful Business
Jeremy L. Spratling
© 2021

All rights reserved. No portion of this book may be reproduced, stored in a retrieval system, or transmitted in any form or by any means—electronic, mechanical, photocopying, recorded, scanning, or other—except for brief quotations in critical reviews or articles, without the prior written permission of the publisher.

As is the nature of the internet, websites change over time. But all websites noted in this book were operational at the time of this writing and were accurately noted to the best of our ability.

ISBN: 978-0997431896

Printed in the United States of America.

CONTENTS

Introduction   vii

Getting Started   11

Structuring Your Business   29

Paying for It   45

Figuring Out Regulations   61

Creating Your Network of Support   73

Building Your Brand   85

Attracting and Keeping Customers   101

Growing Your Business   115

INTRODUCTION

Why did I start my own business? The short answer is to control my destiny.

Like you, I have worked my share of regular 8-5 jobs, and I discovered the glass ceiling is real. I could be the smartest, hardest working person at the company, but that did not necessarily guarantee I would get the promotion. I grew tired of office politics, and I became frustrated because I could not control the trajectory of my own success or determine how far I could advance.

But I did not waste those opportunities. Before becoming a business owner, I worked for blue-chip brokerage and banking firms for almost two decades, and I had many first-rate on-the-job learning opportunities. I used my time at those companies to learn all I could on their dime, and I took those experiences with me when I became a business owner.

Introduction

I worked in private wealth management, taught classes for many years, and then moved into corporate finance. I asked questions, took classes, observed how those companies established and operated their systems, figured out how to find and source money, discovered how successful business owners handle their personal and company assets, and learned how deals are made. These opportunities put me in contact with influential people with high net worth and executives who run large corporations. When I became a business owner, I had a head start with an abundance of experiences and information.

Small-business ownership is America's number one way to grow. It is crucial to the nation's economy and to individual wealth. For most people, it is almost impossible to reach a high net worth working a regular job. They are not able to provide wealth for themselves, and they are not able to build generational wealth for their families. But when they become business owners, they can chart their own destiny, build wealth, provide for their families, and mentor and give back to others who could benefit from their knowledge and experience.

My purpose for writing this book is to help you to prepare to become a successful business owner and to answer many of your "how?" and "what now?" questions. Although I have an extensive background in working at top-level businesses and in the fields of finance and economics, I still did a lot of guessing when I first started. For people who do not have a similar background, owning a business must seem daunting and overwhelming. I want to remove some of that guesswork.

There is a wealth of information out there for beginning entrepreneurs, but each person's experiences are unique. I want to share with you the knowledge I gained after working in corporate America for a couple of decades before becoming an entrepreneur and owning my own business—what worked, what did not work, information to get you started, help with speaking the language of business, and roadblocks to look out for. I also want to challenge you to ask yourself the tough questions every potential business owner needs to ask.

On my road to business ownership, I went left when I should have gone right, and I have made some detours along the way. I have been through many of the situations you will inevitably face. When I mentor other business owners, I always tell them to take advice only from someone who has been in business for many years and has gone through similar situations. Anything else is just opinions and guesses at best.

If you are taking a leap of faith and going from a regular job to becoming a business owner, congratulations! You have just decided to control your own destiny and to go further than you could ever go working for someone else. As you prepare to become an entrepreneur, I will help you navigate the choppy waters and share valuable insight and encouragement along the way.

CHAPTER 1

GETTING STARTED

I applaud you for wanting to be a business owner. As an executive mentor, I regularly counsel first-time business owners, and I do everything I can to help them reach their goals. They are go-getters who are ready to leave their regular jobs behind and have something of their own, a means of building wealth and controlling their own destiny. But before you take this plunge, make sure you are prepared. It is not a journey for the faint of heart. Being your own boss takes discipline, drive, and determination. But it also means a lot of paperwork and attention to detail. You do not want to sideline your business before you even get started, so let us walk through what you can expect as you prepare yourself to own a business.

What Is Your Driven Purpose?

Some people believe that when they start a business, they have to go into an area they are passionate about, an area they love.

I do not believe that.

There are plenty of things you like to do, and you might even be able to operate a business based on any of those interests—for a while—but you need more than your passion to motivate you. If you think back, you can probably remember several passions you have had that came and went. But those things you are driven to achieve do not fade away, and they are not superseded by other passions and interests.

I am not discouraging your passion for your business. It is possible to have a passion for what you do and be successful, but it is not required. Often, we may be passionate about hobbies or interests, and we are good at them; but we may not be able to turn them into successful businesses.

YOUR AHA MOMENT

Something else that works hand in hand with your driven purpose is your *aha moment*. Perhaps you have had one or more of these. An *aha moment* is when an idea for a product or service hits you. It is not just a passing thought, but it is more like a fire burning inside that will not allow you to forget it until you try to make it happen. Your aha moment can make you a trailblazer and create an avenue to make your idea available to the public. You are intensely focused on it, no matter what obstacles get in the way.

For example, you might love to cook and prepare meals your whole family loves. You might become a chef in a restaurant and do a good job of putting delicious food on the plates of happy customers. But your skills and talents as a cook or a chef do not guarantee you will be good at owning and running a restaurant. The skills you need to cook are not the same as the ones you will need to run a successful business.

You have to ask yourself if you can do what you love and handle all the aspects of the business that would need to be built around it every single day, not just when the business is going well or when you feel like it. If your answer is no, that is a sign you should not base your business on your passion.

When you first start out, you will have more ugly days than pretty ones. One day may be a good day, but you may lose ten sales the next day. You might not be able to deal with that, and you will need concrete reasons and real purpose to motivate you. Your purpose has to drive you to work in the intense heat of summer or the bitter cold of winter. It will make you sit up all night to finish a proposal you have for a morning meeting.

I would encourage you to discover your driven purpose and build your business on it. Every successful entrepreneur has something that drives him or her to deal with the ups and downs of owning a business. I will share with you my driven purpose.

My number one motivation is strictly financial. That might sound crass or greedy to you, but it is what gets me up in the morning and makes me sacrifice for my business in the ways I do.

I own a facility services business. We offer a range of building management services. Do I love that particular field? Not necessarily. But I do enjoy owning my own business, which offers me flexibility that working a regular job would not. I know all of my financial needs will be met because I provide a great service and make good money doing it.

If you ask most entrepreneurs why they started their businesses, you will get a variety of answers. These are the most common:

- Some people go into business for the **status**. They like the glitz and glamor of being at the top and telling other people they own a business. They believe business ownership confers on them a special status they would not get working a regular job.

- Business owners enjoy the **freedom** of being their own boss. They control their destiny because there is no one to tell them what to do. While owning a business is hard work, it also gives them the flexibility an 8-5 job does not give them.

- People want to improve their **finances**. Many business owners are looking to build generational wealth for their families, and they want to make the amount of money they know they would not make if they were working for someone else.

Another thing that drives me is a fear of failure. I am terrified to go back to what I was before, to go backward. Your fear may drive you to the challenges of owning a business or drive you away from it. Some days, I wake up thinking, *What if every contract is canceled today?* That is unlikely to happen, but it is something I have to think about. I am not driven by any particular passions. I am driven not to be poor and to work so my children will have wealth.

Before you dive into business ownership, figure out why you want to be an entrepreneur. If your reason rests solely on an intense passion, perhaps you need to give yourself more time to discover your driven purpose.

PASSION VS. PROFIT

Businesses have to turn a profit to survive, so running solely on passion is one of the fastest ways to fail. I had an associate who was passionate about going into business. Her reason? She wanted to provide a place for employees to work where they would love their jobs and like her as their boss. She wanted her employees to have the greatest work experience in the world. When I asked her about the product or service she would provide, she let me know those were not her focus at all. Perhaps she should have spent more time focusing on products and profit over passion because she no longer has a business.

Her passion for creating a friendly work environment was noble and inspiring, but it was not sustainable. It was not enough to keep her business afloat because it finally slammed up against the reality of any business: the entrepreneur's focus on the product or services he or she provides.

ASK YOURSELF

Why do I want to start a business?

Am I prepared to walk away from an 8-5 job?

Can I deal with not having health insurance for a while until I can build up my company and provide it for myself and my family? How will not having insurance affect my family? Will my family support my decision?

Am I prepared to work 12-, 16-, or 18-hour days on a regular basis?

Can I handle the stress of clients calling me when things are not right?

Can I handle the stress of not making sales for several weeks or months at a time?

WHO ARE YOU?

Small-business Dreamer: You dream of starting a business, and you have been telling everyone for years that one day you will own your own business. But you have not gotten very far. You have a great idea in mind, and all of your plans are in your head, but you have not written anything down. You daydream of being free from the constraints of your regular job, and you have done some surface-level research on getting started; but it has been ten years, and nothing has happened. You keep waiting for the perfect time and perfect circumstances, which will never happen, so you keep dreaming that one day . . .

Self-employed: You actually took a leap of faith and started your own business. But after several years, you notice you are just spinning your wheels. You are working for the business instead of the business working for you. You are not advancing or growing. Maybe you lack a vision for the future. If you are honest, when you think about how things are going, you might as well be working for someone else. You are not controlling your destiny or enjoying the freedom of business ownership. Before you know it, it will be time for you to retire and ride off into the sunset, and you will not have achieved any of your entrepreneurial goals.

Business Owner: You have the kind of business you want, and it is going the way you planned for it to go. You are managing the business efficiently and managing your employees effectively. You are guiding the way for the business, and you are in control. At the same time, you are having fun with it and enjoying the personal and financial freedom it affords you. After a few years of entrepreneurship, you are starting to see the fruits of your labor, the progress you have worked hard for. You stay on top of your profit and loss statements, your taxes, and your financial information; and you regularly check and revise your business plan. You network and make connections in order to advance and grow your business.

Procrastinating. The idea of starting a business sounds good, but putting in the work can be daunting to a lot of people, and they put it off. "I will start next week," but by the time next week rolls around, they are not ready. Then they put it off until the first of the year or after their children get into college or after. . . . Then five years have passed, and nothing has happened. Wrong mindset. Fear drives me to do my best, but it does not control me. I use it to motivate me. But you can get stuck in fear and never reach your potential, which is the difference between a small-business dreamer and a business owner.

Start Where You Are

As a mentor, I advise college students who are considering the path to entrepreneurship it is okay to start out in corporate America before they own a business. If that is where you are, then I want to show you why it is a good idea to go that route.

If you are graduating from college and looking for a job, or you are already working for a company, learn as much as you can wherever you are. At the very least, you will learn what *not* to do. But you will gain valuable skills and lessons that will serve you well in the future. You can get free, in-depth training on the job, which will help prepare you for your future role as an entrepreneur.

Observe how things are done at your company, how they create and manage their processes, how their systems are established. Many companies offer free classes, seminars, and training sessions. If it is a successful company, you can be assured the training will be of good quality.

Do not be discouraged by the monotony of your job. Use it as a learning opportunity. It may seem to you as if you are doing the same thing every day, but the monotony is what helps to develop your dedication and work ethic. Think of it as chopping wood. If you need wood, chopping wood becomes a chore you do regularly to ensure you have enough wood to burn and not run out. You chop wood, knowing what you are doing may be boring and monotonous, but it is a necessary task to keep you and your family warm.

Many of the regular jobs you hold may feel like the repetitive chore of chopping wood but, then again, so are the responsibilities of being a business owner There are daily chores you will have that, though repetitive, are crucial to the smooth running of your business. You have to make calls, go the post office, do payroll, and return calls and emails. Just keep in mind, by doing these crucial tasks steadily and regularly over and over, you will be more successful.

As you are learning the basics of business where you are, also focus on your work ethic. You will need to be more committed to your business than you are now to your regular job. If you are struggling with discipline—getting to work on time, completing projects, forming relationships with team members—start working on those habits before you take on business ownership.

There will be days when you will have things you do not want to do, but if you want your business to be successful, you will need to do them anyway. You might need to take on jobs and responsibilities you do not like, but in the beginning, it may be necessary. In the beginning, I took on jobs I would never take on now. But those are the jobs that paid the bills, gave me the experience I needed, and helped me to get parts of my business up and running.

While I was working for other people, I learned discipline and a great work ethic. I get up at 4:15 every morning, and I usually do not go to bed until 11:00 at night. That leaves me plenty of time to get it all done. There are times when I would rather sleep in, but I know if I do not get up and get moving, nothing will get done. I learned that if someone has to push you, you are going to find it hard to be disciplined. You will have to find ways to motivate yourself.

Use this time wisely to train yourself to be the type of business owner you want to be. You will be glad you did.

Business Plan

Some people would say your business plan is your road map to success. But road maps—while good—are old-school. They are static and, once printed, they can become obsolete. I would say your business plan is more like a GPS. A GPS, when connected, will always give you the latest and most current route for you to take. It is constantly updated so you can avoid road construction, route changes, and accidents.

Because your business plan is a living document, it is not carved in stone and forever preserved in a case and placed upon a shelf. Actually, you should revisit your business plan regularly to change and update it as needed.

When creating a business plan, do not stress out about it. Think of it as a handy set of guidelines to get you started. Although you want a plan with solid, detailed information, this is not your high school term paper or college thesis. It does not have to contain hundreds of pages with footnotes.

The purpose of your business plan is to help you see if your proposed business ideas are ones you really want to pursue. It will help you to lay out more clearly what you want to do and how you plan to achieve your goals. It forces you to think about whether your ideas are viable or if they are just fantasies. Developing your plan makes you write out the inner workings of your business and what it will look like and forces you to size up your competition and how much money you will need to be competitive.

I recommend you pull out your business plan every few months, or once a quarter, and see if you are on track with what you said you would do or if anything needs to be changed. You can always revise your plan based on your day-to-day reality, and you can make decisions accordingly.

WORD TO THE WISE

Do not pay anyone else to do your business plan for you. You might think it would be easier and faster. Maybe. But paying someone else to write your plan for you will not give you, the business owner, the same depth or insight into your business. Doing it yourself means you have to do the research. If you are not good with numbers, you will be when you have to come up with them for your business plan. By writing your own business plan, you will learn a lot more and gain a wealth of knowledge you are going to need.

ASK YOURSELF

What are my long-term business goals for the next five years? ten years?

How much income can I generate over the next year? five years? ten years?

How do I want my life and my business to look after five years? ten years?

Will my business allow me to build wealth for myself and leave a legacy for my family?

Plan for Growth Now

And while you are planning, go ahead and plan for growth. Yes, you are just starting out, but it will not hurt to plan for the future. Look ahead and think of how you want to grow, what your growth will look like, and how that might be sustainable.

Then when you get started, set aside some time every day to plan for growth. Every time you make money, do not blow it all by celebrating. Save a portion of what you are not currently putting into the business. I have saved money since day one, and I encourage you to do the same. You never know when a big contract will come your way, and you need to be prepared for it. Potential clients will not wait several weeks or months while you scramble to get the money together to fill their orders. They will simply move on to the next company that can accommodate their needs.

When business is going well, you will need more inventory and possibly more staff. You will also want to think about how you can increase your profits. For example, if you make $10,000 this year but you want to do $50,000 next year, map out how you plan to do that. Make your future part of your business plan now so you can be adequately prepared.

Research

Before you rush to offer your products or services in the marketplace, do your research. Find out what the market is for what you want to offer. Just because you are excited about your products and services does not mean anyone else will be. If your products and services are what you are going to hang your shingle on and provide your future livelihood, then you will need to do extensive research before you open your doors.

- **Online.** This is probably where most people start their research. It is relatively easy, and it is free. But do not limit yourself to online resources. There is a wealth of knowledge outside of cyberspace that could benefit you.

- **Libraries.** Go old-school. While there is a lot of good information online, you have to be careful and know the

ORGANIZATIONS THAT CAN HELP

Besides friends and mentors, there are organizations that specialize in offering free help and other resources to small-business owners.

Small Business Administration (SBA), established in 1953, is a federal agency that offers a variety of resources to small businesses so they can "confidently start, grow, expand, and recover." To learn more, go to **sba.gov/**.

SCORE is a resource partner of the SBA and has offered education and mentorship to small businesses since 1964. To learn more, go to **score.org/**.

difference between what is good, solid information and what is faulty information or someone's opinion. Read books written by successful people who have been where you want to go. When you are first starting out, you probably do not have a lot of money to spend on expensive Business 101-type books. Go online, look up book titles that interest you, and find those books at your local library. Librarians can also recommend good titles for you.

- **College students.** You could conduct studies with students in their classes for market research. The research will let you know if your product or service is viable in a particular area or if there is a brand-new product no one has seen before.

- **Mentors and other business owners.** Some of your best resources will be people who have done, or are presently doing, what you want to do. You may find some of them already in your circle of influence, or you can seek out business organizations such as the Small Business Administration or SCORE for help with research.

As a mentor and a SCORE counselor, I encourage you to use all the resources available to you, especially those organizations that are geared to new business owners. When I wanted to expand my company's services to include security, I asked a friend to recommend someone I could talk with who had experience in that field. She knew someone who owned a security company and put me in touch. When I connected with him, he gave me so much information, I could not write it all down. He kindly invited me to call him if I needed help with anything. He made himself an open resource for me. To this day, I stay in contact with him.

Lacking information. When people come to me to get advice on starting a business, the first question I ask is, "Have you set up an LLC?" Often, they give me a blank look and ask, "What is an LLC?" When you have not done your research, you do not know what you do not know.

Acting on bad advice. You will need to discern good advice from bad advice. Do not talk to just one person. Instead, seek out as many people as you can who will be willing to help, and then take a consensus of the advice you have been given. Ultimately, you are the one making the decisions, and you will have to deal with the consequences.

ASK YOURSELF

Is my product or service being offered by other companies? If so, how big is the market for my product or service?

What is the going rate for what I want to offer?

Can I be competitive?

Will I be competing with mom-and-pop companies or big-box corporations?

Should I offer it locally, nationally, internationally?

CHAPTER 2

STRUCTURING YOUR BUSINESS

How you structure your business is essential and will become the foundation on which you will build everything else. The structure you build now will determine many of the decisions you will make as a business owner—from how you source your funding to who you choose to hire to how you build your brand. However, when I talk with new business owners, I caution them: If they build the foundation of their business too narrow or too shallow, as their business grows, it will topple and fall. I encourage you to carefully consider how you structure your business from day one, and surround yourself with trusted, competent people who can help you build something that will be successful *and* sustainable in the years to come.

Your Structure Means Everything

When you are planning to start a business, there are several business structures you should consider. Think carefully what you want to achieve and what you want your business to look like. Then talk to your mentor or other business professionals who can advise you on what business structure will work best for you.

If you are going it alone, a one-person operation, then you might want to consider **sole proprietorship**. This is right for you if you are planning to be The Lone Ranger and you do not need any other employees. This business model will make filing your taxes easier. The drawback is if a customer is unhappy with your products or services and wants to take you to court, you are solely and personally responsible for any liabilities.

If you are selling a product, it would be better for you to have a **limited liability company (LLC)**, the most common type of structure. If you go this route, you are probably going to have other employees, equipment, and company vehicles. Forming an LLC will protect you from any possible liabilities because your company is now its own entity. If someone wants to take you to court, they can only sue the company or go after your company's assets, not your personal assets. You will not be held personally liable for any damages.

If you decide to take on a business partner, consider a **limited liability partnership** (**LLP**). Forming an LLP better defines your brand and specifies the roles you and your business partner will play in the operation of the company. When I mentor potential business owners, I advise them to form an LLP if they are going into partnership because it is important to have every detail of your business agreement written down to make sure each partner's duties are recorded and well-defined. It also provides a level of protection because if a partner is negligent in his or her duties or commits misconduct and someone sues, then only the guilty partner will be responsible and will be sued, not you.

Unlike an LLC or an LLP, a **subchapter S company** does not pay taxes. Profits roll over to the owners, and they pay taxes on the amount they take out. For example, if I put $10,000 into my company, I am not taxed on it. I am only taxed on it when I decide to withdraw the money from the company.

A **C Corporation** (**C Corp**) "is a separate legal entity set up under state law" that protects you from assets from creditor claims. If you choose to incorporate your business, it becomes a C Corp. Your business will then be "a separate taxpayer, with income and expenses taxed to the corporation" and not to you. "If corporate profits are then distributed to owners as dividends, owners must pay personal income tax on the distribution, creating "double taxation." For this reason, you probably will not want to use this model as a new business owner.[1]

Business Structures Compared[1]

	Sole Proprietor	Limited Liability Company (LLC)	Limited Liability Partnership (LLP)	S Corp	C Corp
Formation	No filing required	No filing required	State filing required	State filing required	State filing required
Limited personal liability	No	No	Yes	Yes	Yes, except for own malpractice
Transferability of interest	No	No	Yes	Generally Limited	Generally Limited
Duration	Until withdrawal or death of owner	Unlimited	Unlimited	Unlimited	Unlimited
Pass-through taxation	Yes	Yes	No	Yes	No
Ability to raise capital	Not as separate entity	Yes	Yes	Yes, but shareholder limits	Yes
Limitations on number of owners	Yes	No	No	Yes	No, but all owners must be part of same profession

Partnerships

When I first became an entrepreneur, I had business partners.

It did not end well.

Money was spent, and commitments were made, but my business partners did not live up to their agreements. Be cautious before entering into business partnerships. When I advise potential business owners, I recommend the following:

Know who you are dealing with. Seems simple enough. Hopefully, you know the person well enough to feel comfortable going into business together, but there is nothing wrong with doing a background check on someone you know, reviewing his or her resume, or having an honest discussion about the person's finances. You have to think about future business projects. What if you need additional funding? If your partner is not dependable to have investments for future projects, you will lose any investments you have made, and your projects will fail.

Also, do not assume because you have known someone for years that he or she will make a perfect business partner. Some people think just because they are going into business with family members or friends everything will be fine. But what they do not consider is a business relationship is different from other types of relationships. If something goes wrong with the business, it will probably affect your friendship or family relationship.

Do not be pressured into a partnership. Business partnerships can be great for starting and growing your business, but they can make business ownership quite complicated. Once you are committed, your name, reputation, and money is on the line; and it can be quite difficult to extricate yourself from it once you have said yes. If you are feeling pressured or pushed into a partnership you do not feel comfortable with, slow down and take time to think it over. Talk about it with your mentor or other trusted people before you rush into anything. If you have a bad feeling about a potential partner or partnership arrangement, do not be afraid to walk away from it.

Write down what each person will be responsible for—and not responsible for. Be specific about each person's duties, including financial responsibilities, and put it in writing. Then make sure everyone signs off on it to confirm everyone is in agreement. Written agreements leave no gray areas. In some of the business agreements I have been in, I have used a *letter of understanding*, which lays out how our shared projects will look, what each of us is committing to, and the parameters of our partnership. This agreement can also specify the partners' financial responsibilities. Who will sign, or not sign, the checks? Who can indebt the company? Consult with your attorney and mentors to advise you on best practices.

Negotiate the financial part of your partnership up front. Decide if you will have an equal partnership or if you will have a partner who will invest only a percentage of the capital you need. Think carefully about how much control and equity of your business you will be willing to give up as your company grows. (You might also consider a silent partnership. See Chapter 3 for more on silent partnerships.)

Have an exit strategy. Even with the best of intentions, some partnerships just do not work well. Have an exit strategy in place for you and your business partner(s) so you can get out of the deal as quickly as possible and protect yourself and your assets if things go sour. When you are writing your letter of understanding, or operating agreement, insert a sales clause. This clause will allow any of the partnering parties to exit the arrangement at any time, but it allows the remaining parties to have *right of first refusal*.

RIGHT OF FIRST REFUSAL

According to SmallBusiness.Chronicle.com, "the right of first refusal, . . . gives the holder the right to review all other offers on a business or share of a business. The holder of the right can buy the business simply by matching the highest offer on the table. Businesses partners often grant each other the right of first approval. In those cases, when a partner wants out of the business, the remaining partners can prevent a newcomer they do not know from buying a stake in the firm."[2] The party leaving a partnership must offer his or her shares/equity at a predetermined price. If the remaining parties refuse them, the leaving party can sell them to someone else.

Your operating agreement can also designate if the partnership dissolves, you and your partner(s) can shut down the company and liquidate the assets. The operating agreement would specify what would happen after the liquidation.

Wanting a partnership for the wrong reasons. Partnerships can be a great way for your business to grow. But if you are not a good fit for taking on a partner and you are just doing it for the money a partner brings to the table, that will be a recipe for disaster.

Not doing your due diligence. If you know your partner, great, but you still need to do your homework. Once you get into a partnership, you might find yourself entangled in deals you may be personally responsible for if your partner walks away, and you might run into serious legal issues.

Not having a Plan B. You can plan for the future, but you never know if it will all work out. As an effective business owner, you always need a Plan B. Even in a good partnership, you need a way out if things do not work. Without an exit strategy, you may be putting your business at risk.

ASK YOURSELF

Do I find it easy to work with other people? Why or why not?

Do I have a good feeling about working with a potential partner? Why? If not, what are my reservations?

Am I a good listener?

How do I respond to criticism?

If I am considering a partnership, do I have a letter of understanding or an operating agreement?

Do I have an exit strategy?

Getting the Best Employees

Unless you are planning to go it alone, you are going to need a staff of employees; and this is a crucial step in structuring your business. But finding the right employees can be difficult. We probably all know of people who hate their jobs or people who are not proficient at their jobs, and they offer horrible customer service and make the company they work for look bad. How do you find and keep the best employees? That is the million-dollar question.

In many ways, the nuts and bolts of running your business is the easy part compared to recruiting and keeping good staff. And employees make running a business more complicated, to say the least. In an ideal world, employees would clock in, do the jobs they are paid to do—not even over and beyond or amazingly, just what they agreed to do—clock out, and go home. But that is not real life.

In reality, some of the employees you will hire will have personal matters they will bring to work with them, thus reducing their productivity; they will struggle with substance abuse; they may have unresolved legal issues; they will have childcare concerns; they might be apathetic toward their jobs; and, like most people, they will have good days and bad days. Hiring good employees is often a matter of chance, but there are steps you can take to ensure you get a better quality of employees.

I will start with the most obvious: **Carefully review employees' resumes, call and speak with their references, and do background checks.** There is no substitute for doing your due diligence and checking to make sure your employees are who they say they are and their qualifications are solid. Do not skip this obvious but crucial step, even with people you think you know or who come highly recommended. This step acts as a safety net for you and your company and will help weed out many of the unsuitable candidates from the start. But even after taking this step, you still might have employees who do not live up to expectations, so here are a few other steps you can take to hire good employees:

Ask your best, most trusted employees if they know anyone who could work for you. Good current employees are a great resource for good future employees. Typically, good employees are not going to recommend other people who are going to mess up on the job because they do not want to jeopardize their name and reputation. Also, good employees care about your company, they know your expectations as the business owner, and they are already familiar with the company's requirements.

Look carefully at how long potential employees have worked at past jobs. More specifically, look at the amount of time they have held each job. Are they job-hoppers? If so, why? Did they get fired? Did they leave for better opportunities and higher pay? For example, if a person has had ten jobs in the last six years, and he or she worked each job for only six or seven months, that is a red flag. That person is probably not going to stick around at your company either. It is difficult to run a business when your employee turnover rate is high and changes every six months.

Be extremely clear about *everything*. Make sure employees get a copy of company policies and your expectations for employees, and make sure they sign off on *everything*. This provides protection for you as well as for them. More important, employees cannot come to you later and say they did not know or did not understand their duties and what you expect from them.

Document *everything*. Keep good employee records. In case you face legal issues, you will have clear documentation, and it will make things easier to defend yourself and your company.

Observe how employees get along with other employees. Unfortunately, there are some things you will not know about someone until after he or she is hired. One thing you should observe right after that person is hired is how he or she interacts with fellow employees. Of course, you want employees to do a good job. But if they cannot get along with their fellow employees, their performance and the performance of other employees will eventually suffer, and it will give you more headaches when you have to deal with it.

Being too cheap to invest in the security and well-being of your company. Do not cut corners on background checks and record-keeping. The money and time you invest up front for these services and tasks will save you much more later on.

BACKGROUND CHECKS

As an employer, you will need to perform background checks on potential employees to make sure you are getting the best and most trusted people on your team. Most basic background checks include a person's education, work history, criminal record, and drug screening. If you need more information, you can elect to conduct a more advanced check. Research different background-check services offering the information you need at the price you can afford. While there are free services available, invest in a quality service that will give you current and accurate information.

ASK YOURSELF

What specific needs do I have for potential employees?

Do I have an employee manual that is clearly written? If so, is it specific about company expectations and practices? Is it up-to-date?

How will I document and record my hiring process and employee interactions?

Your Construction Crew

A good construction crew includes skilled people who perform specialized jobs in order to build a safe structure that meets regulations and building codes. As a business owner, you also need to surround yourself with a crew of people who will help you not only to build your business, but to help you maintain and keep it in good working order for the long-term. It will cost you a little more money on the front end, but it will save you headaches down the road.

Accountant: An accountant should be the first person you bring onto your crew. He or she can answer your financial questions, but your accountant can also advise you on certain legal matters, make sure you are compliant with various regulations, and recommend other professionals you might need to consult.

Mentor: A good mentor for a business owner should be someone who has experience in the field, but he or she is not just a sounding board for you. Your mentor will be willing to invest time and resources to help you and advise you on real-world problems you will encounter.

Attorney: You may consult with an attorney only once or twice a year, but he or she will be essential to your crew. While I do not recommend you keep an attorney on retainer in the beginning, it is good to know someone who is qualified to handle legal matters unique to your type of business.

Banker: Once your company grows, your financial needs will grow. If you have developed a relationship with your banker, he or she will know your story and how to best meet your needs. Also, a banker will feel more comfortable negotiating terms with you if you have regular contact and have a good record with the bank.

Supplier: Find a good supplier, and build a relationship so that as you grow, you can negotiate prices and services. When your supplier can offer what you need when you need it, it makes you look good because you are able to deliver the goods and services to your customers and keep your promises.

If you are struggling to find people to work with you as you build your business, talk with those closest to you first. Your family members and friends may know qualified people who can be part of your team or recommend others who will be willing to help and support you. Then talk with your local chamber of commerce and the Better Business Bureau for references and ratings of trusted professionals in your area.

CHAPTER 3

PAYING FOR IT

You are probably trying to figure out where you will get the money to start your business. If you do not have a lot of money in your bank account then, yes, you will need to acquire funding from somewhere. You may be worried you will not get the funding you need to start the business of your dreams, or you are anxious about the mountains of paperwork you will need to complete. I coach many potential entrepreneurs through the funding process, and some of them think they will apply for grants and get "free" money or apply for bank loans. If that is what you are thinking, I have some good news and bad news for you. The bad news is you probably will not get a grant (for reasons I will explain later). But the good news is you are not limited to traditional bank loans. As someone who has worked in banking and economics and as a fellow business owner, I am thrilled to tell you there is a plethora of options for you to choose from. But there are also crucial details you will need to consider. In this chapter, you will discover one or more options that will work for you.

Preparing to Meet With Lenders

Map out what kind of business you are going to have because that is going to determine the "how?" and "where?" of your funding. Is your business service-based or product-based? If it is service-based, you are selling intellectual labor or labor that is not necessarily tangible, for example, accounting services, legal work, or even janitorial services. Your funding needs will be lower because

WHAT WOULD YOU SAY?

Talking cogently about your business will be a key factor in securing funding. Before you meet with lenders, practice talking about your business with your friends or mentor. I once mentored someone who was just starting out. He said he would not have to tell anybody about his business because his service spoke for itself. I told him he could be the best personal trainer in the world, but if he could not tell anybody about it, he would have zero sales and he would ultimately fail. No matter how good he thought he was at his business, how would other people know if he did not tell them?

you will need less inventory, if any at all. But if you are offering products—for example, sofas, automotive parts, or widgets—you will need inventory, somewhere to store the inventory, machinery, and other equipment. Find a lender who understands what you do and can meet your needs.

Build or repair your personal credit. Your personal credit does not have to be perfect, but it cannot be so low that you appear completely untrustworthy. Lenders will have no choice but to turn you down. It may not sound fair, but they will assume if you cannot handle your own finances, you probably will not do a good job managing your company's finances and will not repay the loan, and they will not be willing to take the risk. Pull your credit report, and see if there is anything you can clean up before you apply for funding for your business. If you need to work with trusted professionals to help you with your credit, it will be worth it.

Create a personal financial statement. Lenders will want to know what personal assets you have and will want to use them as collateral for any loan money you might receive. Since you are starting a new business, you are not going to have any business assets, so lenders will need to collateralize your personal assets.

If you have had any business experience and you have a profit and loss statement, make it as detailed as you can, to the penny. You can use your profit and loss statement to show on a month-to-month basis, you made money and handled it responsibly. This will give you traction and make it easier to get the financing you need.

Familiarize yourself with the ins and outs of your future business. You will need to put all that information on paper and be able to articulate it clearly to lenders. You can have the greatest business idea in the world, but if you cannot explain it clearly enough to someone else, it will be difficult to find lenders who will want to invest in you.

After you create your business plan, hire someone to review it. You want to make sure your business plan is neat and clear. In my banking career, I read hundreds of business plans. Some were amazingly written; others, not so much. Your business plan is part of the first impression of yourself you will present to potential lenders. If your business plan is messy, filled with typos, and unclear, lenders will discredit your abilities to run a business.

Meet with your accountant. Let your accountant look over your numbers to make sure they align with your business plan. Together you can determine what percentage of money should go to personnel, salaries, vendors, inventory, or equipment, for example. Also, gather any financial documents you may need, such as your tax returns.

When You Meet With Lenders

Before you meet with lenders, you need to articulate for yourself how much funding you need and what you will do with it. You could include a source and uses statement in your business plan to help make it clear. The funding you are requesting might be for marketing, media, or maintenance; but your figures have to add up to match what you are asking for and how much, and it has to make sense. Lenders want to see that the money will be used for operational expenses. Needless to say, the money cannot go for your personal vacation to Maui or to put a down payment on a Tesla. It must go directly into the business.

Lenders will deeply scrutinize your business plan. I mentioned in Chapter 1 that your business plan is a living document, and it will need to be checked and revised regularly. Your plan will tell the lender you understand what you are getting into and if there are any hiccups along the way, you are prepared. Consider including a source and uses statement in your plan to help you articulate that. It would also include pro-forma projections, details about realistic incremental gains, and a map for growth. Lenders will want to see you have done your homework and you are serious about what you want to do.

Sources and uses statement: This statement shows where "all the sources of funds for a project come from, and where all those funds are used in a project."[1]

Pro-forma projection: This is a financial forecast "based on pro-forma income statements, balance sheets, and cash flow statements."[2]

ASK YOURSELF

Can I articulate what my business is about in a way that would help lenders understand my financial needs and encourage them to take a risk?

Do I have all of my financials together?

Do I have all of my important documents ready for lenders to review?

How detailed is my business plan? Does it include everything I will need to show lenders?

Lending Sources

Traditional bank financing. This is the place where many people think they have to start. If you do go this route, you will need all of your paperwork in order, and you will need to be aware of your personal credit score. While this is still a legitimate way for small business owners to get started, it is by far not the only—or the best—way for many people to get the funding they need. Instead, consider the following:

Community development corporations (CDC). These lending institutions are found in large urban cities, small rural towns, and economically depressed areas. These areas might receive grant money to fund small businesses or minority-owned businesses to help them grow. CDCs are usually nonprofit businesses, and they specialize in providing capital at reasonable terms to small or micro businesses.

Angel investors. These types of investors are usually wealthy people who come together as a group to lend money to small businesses. I know someone whose company was bought by angel investors. Then he started his own angel investment group in Birmingham.

Venture capitalists. Venture capitalists are always looking to invest, but they are looking for equity out of your company. They are not as likely to loan money because they know you could probably go to the bank and get a loan. They want equity if they see potential in your company. As your company grows, their stake grows in value.

Partner financing, or joint venture partner financing. This is a trend in many industries that can be mutually beneficial. For example, if you want to start a janitorial service, you could partner with a much larger janitorial services company. The larger company would help you get started, which is obviously beneficial to you, but you might wonder how it is beneficial to the larger company. Some government contracts require large companies to partner with smaller companies to help them grow. If you are a minority-owned small business, the larger company can claim the minority business designation because a portion of their profits are helping a small minority-owned business. So, by entering into such partnerships, the benefit to larger companies is that they are then eligible for more lucrative contracts.

Invoice financing. This is not my favorite source of funding, but I have included it so you have access to as many sources as possible and to share with you the pros and cons of funding. Let us say you need $10,000 to do work for a contract for services, but you do not have it. Some companies will give you $8,000. When you get paid by your customer, your lender will take a percentage of your revenue right off the top. That arrangement will continue as long as you work with the lender. This source is okay if you need funding quickly and cannot wait 30 to 90 days for your invoice to be paid.

Grants. Many of the people I mentor let me know up front they are interested in getting grants to start their businesses. I hate to disappoint them, but business grants are far and few in between when it comes to for-profit businesses. Typically, grants are more commonly given for science and research facilities. Sometimes small businesses in economically depressed areas can get grants; but if you are opening your business in any average American city, you are probably not going to get a grant. The SBA offers a few grants for innovation research and business technology organizations. If that is your business plan, then you might benefit from that source.

Family and friends. Do not overlook the sources closest to you. It never hurts to ask your family members and friends to invest in you. Perhaps they will see potential in your business, understand your vision, and believe in you enough to give you some—if not all—of the money you need.

Merchant cash advance. This type of funding occurs when your financial provider sends you a lump sum of money to finance the products you have. For example, if you own a restaurant and you run $10,000 worth of sales, it usually takes a few days for the money to hit your account. Your financial provider pulls your receivables and then will send you a PO, a percentage, immediately. Instead of having to wait several days for the money to clear your account, your financial provider will advance you the money. When your money is available, it will not end up in your account. Instead, it will go straight to your financial provider, paying them back for the cash advance.

Micro lenders. Micro lenders are similar to traditional banks, but their sole purpose is to take more risk than your average bank. Thus, their interest rates are typically higher, some of their criteria may be a bit tighter, and the amount they are willing to lend may be lower. But for some small businesses, micro lenders are a more realistic way to obtain funding than more traditional sources. Micro lenders are completely legitimate sources of funding. In fact, some major banks have established micro lending banks that are like sister companies. The advantage of borrowing from micro lenders is your working relationship with them will be closer than that of a major bank, but you will still get the funding you need.

Silent partners. You may be interested in taking on a silent partner, someone who will put up a portion of the money you need, but he or she will not have an active role in running your business. Silent partners are not completely excluded from reviewing your numbers, weekly and monthly reports, and profit and loss statements. They just will not be intimately involved in the day-to-day operations. That can be good or bad. While their investment in your business is great and you receive the funding you need, you may not like the silent part of your partnership. There may be times when you will want their input in the more granular levels of running the business. But if they have limited their role to providing capital, then you are not going to have an active partner you can share the load of business with.

Crowdfunding and co-ops. Crowdfunding is a platform that allows a large number of people to pool their money for a cause. Some small-business owners owe their start to crowdfunding. Today, you can find many crowdfunding platforms on the internet that attract large groups of people from around the world, people you will probably never meet. You could get the seed money needed to get started through the development phase. You can submit your business plan for potential investors to review. You may have anywhere from tens of people to thousands of people who want to invest in your business. The investors would take a small percentage of the company, but it would be a good way to quickly raise funds. Co-ops work in a similar way to crowdfunding programs, but they are usually smaller and local.

Self-funding. Probably the safest, if not the fastest, way to get funding is to self-fund. This is the way I came up with the money to start my business; but, then again, I have always been good at saving money. Having your own money allows you to move differently than when you are getting money from other sources. You are not obligated to anyone, and you will not have that debt hanging over you. You are allowed to grow quicker because debt is not hindering you. Self-funding gives you the freedom to do more with your business, and it gives you peace of mind. To this day, my company still does not have debt.

Another bonus of using your own money: By allowing your accountant to structure the investment correctly, you can consider the money a loan to the company, which can pay you back with interest. It is also a great way to pull money out of your company without being taxed on it.

Unsecured vs. Secured Loans

If you go to more traditional sources for funding, you will hear about unsecured or secured loans. An *unsecured loan* does not require collateral. Your name and good credit history is usually enough to secure your loan. The bank believes you are responsible enough to manage and repay the money they will lend you and your business is strong enough to generate the revenue you will need to repay the loan. You will be personally guaranteeing the loan, and if your business goes under, you will still be held liable for the money you borrowed.

Secured loans are attached to collateral. Different things might serve as collateral for your loan. It might be the building your business is housed in, equipment, cash, or a money-market CD. If you are unable to repay the loan, the bank will seize whatever collateral you put up and sell it. The proceeds would go toward repaying the loan. But you also have to personally guarantee the loan as well. For example, if the bank finances your building for

$100,000 and you default on your loan, the bank will seize your building and sell it. But if they only get $50,000 for the building, you are still liable for the remaining $50,000. The bank can also seize other personal assets: your house, your car, or anything in your name.

Comparing Financial Options[1]

Best Small Business Financing Options: Quick Comparison

FINANCING METHOD	INTEREST RATES	REPAYMENT PERIOD	SPEED	BEST FOR:
Bank loans	3% to 6%	Five to 10 years	Two to four weeks	Low-cost debt financing; larger financing needs for established businesses
SBA loans	5% to 10%	Five to 25 years	Average of two to three months	Financing for established businesses that can't qualify for a bank loan
Invoice financing	1% to 3% factor fee per week	Until customer pays invoice	As fast as one day	Debt-based financing that frees capital tied up in unpaid invoices
Merchant cash advances	1.14 to 1.18 factor fee	Paid daily or weekly from your credit card sales	As fast as the same day	Debt financing for businesses who can't qualify for other options
Investors or venture capital	N/A	N/A	Three to nine months	Startup businesses with high and fast growth potential
Friends and family	Depends on your agreement	Varies based on your agreement	Depends on your agreement	Business owners with friends or family willing to support their business financially; those having trouble accessing traditional financing
Crowdfunding	N/A	N/A	Varies based on when people contribute to your campaign	Product-based businesses with social media appeal; supplemental financing
Personal savings	N/A	N/A	Immediate access	Business owners with sizable savings, those who can't access traditional financing

Not knowing the type of funding you need. Before you even think about funding, have all your paperwork in order, and know every detail you can about your business. Talk to mentors and others who can help you determine what type of funding you will need. You do not want to get in over your head.

Asking for too much or too little money. If the amount of money you request is not enough, you will have to return to your lender six or eight months later and go through the process all over again. If you get too much, you will be tempted to overspend and pay interest on money you didn't need.

Being clueless about your financials. You need to have a good knowledge of profit and loss statements, balance sheets, and forecasts. These are tools that can help you to determine how much money you will need at any given point in your business ownership.

Do Not Give Up Your Day Job

If you are not able to get all the funding you need, do not give up on your dream of business ownership. You might need to consider a plan that will allow you to operate your business while waiting to fully fund it.

My answer? Keep working your regular job. You might wonder how you could possibly work an 8-5 job and give the needed time to your business. It may not be as hard as you think:

- Work your business on a freelance basis until you can devote more time to it.
- Devote your after-work hours to your business.
- Operate your business on the weekends.
- Leave your regular job, and take on a part-time job.

By continuing to work a full-time or part-time job, you keep a steady and secure stream of revenue coming in until you can make your business a full-time operation that will be financially sustainable.

If you are a veteran, a service-disabled veteran, a woman, or a minority, you may qualify for special loan programs. For women and minorities who are small-business owners, you will need to receive a *minority designation* before you can qualify, which means you need to acquire a special certification designating you as a minority business owner. You can find more information at SCORE's website: https://www.score.org/blog/how-get-certified-minority-owned-business.

Sources for Funding Information
- SBA
- SCORE
- Accountant
- Mentors
- Other business owners
- Small-business resource centers
- College and university development centers
- Local chamber of commerce

CHAPTER 4

FIGURING OUT REGULATIONS

Owning a business means taking on responsibilities you did not have when you worked a regular job. Many of these new responsibilities include taking care of your employees and making sure you are compliant with local, state, and federal government regulations. This is not the part of the process where you will want to take shortcuts or save money. The government does not look kindly on business owners who ignore regulations or avoid paying taxes. As a mentor, I advise first-time business owners to hire a good accountant before they hire their first employee. An accountant can clear up much of the confusion you might have around what is required of you. But until then, let us look at an overview of what you can expect.

Local, State, and Federal Regulations

You will need to consider several levels of requirements, and you do not want to overlook any of them. Governments at the local, state, and federal levels have regulations you must comply with; and there are several sources you can consult to find out what they are.

Start online at the SBA website, which has a wealth of resources available to you. You can get an idea of what is required by learning how to stay legally compliant (https://www.sba.gov/business-guide/manage-your-business/stay-legally-compliant). Then visit the website of the secretary of state for your state to find out more specific requirements. For a quick way to find your state's secretary of state, go to https://www.thebalancesmb.com/secretary-of-state-websites-1201005.

FIRST THINGS FIRST

Before you do anything, register your business to make sure you can do business under that name. You might be surprised how important this first step will be for you. For more information about registering your business, go to the SBA's website: https://www.sba.gov/business-guide/launch-your-business/register-your-business.

You can also visit your county courthouse and ask what type of licenses and business permits are required in your area. If you decide to do business in several cities and states, you will probably need paperwork for each of them. You may be charged a business privilege tax. If you do not have the proper paperwork, the government might not shut down your business, but you may be hit with heavy fines and penalties. Do not take any chances. Contact the government offices in those areas, and find out what they require.

If you are selling a product, most states require you to register with the state and acquire a sales tax license. You will also need a state tax ID number.

On the federal level, you will need to apply for a federal tax ID number, or Employer Identification Number (EIN), which is used to identify a business entity. You can apply for it online through the IRS website at irs.gov. The US Labor Department's website is also a resource for new and small businesses. Go to dol.gov, and search for "New and Small Businesses."

Your accountant will be a valuable resource for navigating government requirements and regulations. Talk with your accountant to find out what paperwork you need, what you need to apply for, and how often you will need to update or renew any permits or licenses.

Overlooking the details. Some people say, "Do not sweat the small stuff," but when you are starting a business, you do have to sweat the small stuff. For example, if you miss paying payroll taxes, you might owe $1,000. But if you keep overlooking it, you may end up owing $5,000.

Not seeking available help. Do not be so quick to start your business that you do not get the information you need. For the most part, information—even good information—is free. You can click a link, you can ask somebody, you can read a book. There are plenty of resources out there to help you, but you will not know what you need if you do not know what you need.

A NAME IS JUST A NAME?

My business partners and I named our company STG Capital Markets because we were putting our capital into different markets. We were not referring to the stock market; it was just a generic name for markets in general. One day, a man from the Alabama Securities and Exchange Commission came to my office. Our company name had come to his attention, and he thought we were dealing in stocks and bonds and marketable securities without registering with his agency. I assured him we were investing in other businesses and in real estate. But the name we chose triggered something in their system, and I was "rewarded" with a visit. The moral of this story? Think carefully about the name you use for your business. Otherwise, you might get a surprise—and unwanted—visit from the government.

ASK YOURSELF

What criteria am I looking for in a good accountant?

Have I registered my business?

Am I prepared to apply for a federal tax ID number?

Have I applied for local, state, and federal licenses and permits? Am I compliant?

Insurance

As with your personal assets, having insurance offers you protection and peace of mind when things go wrong. Two main types of insurance business owners should have are *general liability* and *workers' compensation*. General liability is not legally required, but it is a basic level of protection for you and your company.

Depending on the type and size of your business, you are legally required to have workers' compensation insurance. In Alabama where my business is, if you have five or more employees, including yourself, you will need to carry it. Talk with other people in your industry about forms of insurance you might need to carry for your specific business.

LESSON LEARNED

About a decade ago, a woman sued one of my supervisors for sexual harassment. I did not know my general liability insurance would cover the claim and help me fight the lawsuit. By the time I found out my insurance would cover it, the case had gone too far, and their representatives could not step in to handle it. I was hit for $20,000, and I had to pay up.

On another occasion, a man fell asleep while driving one of our company vehicles. He was at fault, but that didn't matter as far as his claim. His attorney contacted us, and the first thing I did was call worker's compensation. I gave them all of the information about the case. They fought the case for my company, and they ended up settling for around $95,000. That's huge, but the driver was originally suing my company for $2 million, and we would have had to pay it. But because I have workers' compensation insurance and let them handle the case, I saved a lot of money.

General Liability	Workers' Compensation
Covers injuries to a third party or damage to their property	Covers injuries to employees
Protects third parties	Protects employees
Covers legal fees in suits brought by a third party	Covers legal fees in suits brought by an injured employee
Not legally required, but often contractually required	Legally required
Not regulated	Regulated at the state level[1]

DO NOT MESS WITH UNCLE SAM!

In the Birmingham area, the owner of a large hair salon cheated the federal government out of over a million dollars in payroll taxes. When the government discovered the discrepancy, they did not try to negotiate with him or work out a payment plan. They closed his business and put him in jail because not paying payroll taxes is a federal crime. Lesson learned. Do not try to cheat Uncle Sam!

DO YOUR HOMEWORK

The Internal Revenue Service (IRS) offers an abundance of information about being tax compliant. Your accountant will be helpful in pointing you to useful documents and walking you through what you need to know. One helpful document is the Employer's Tax Guide, which offers information on employee social security numbers, family employees, wages and tips, wage withholdings, earned income credit (EIC), and tax help. To download a copy of this guide, go to https://www.irs.gov/pub/irs-pdf/p15.pdf.

BETTER BUSINESS BUREAU

The Better Business Bureau (BBB) is a great platform for small business owners. They give you a forum to register your business, receive ratings, and dispute any customer complaints. The BBB will offer mediation services before legal matters go to court. It allows potential buyers or clients to know how many years you have been with the BBB and what your BBB rating is. If you maintain a good rating, it gives you credibility in the marketplace. It is also a good resource for referrals. In fact, some of my clients have found me because of the BBB. For more information, visit their website: https://www.bbb.org/.

Figuring Out Regulations

What are my business insurance needs?

Am I familiar with the protection and services my insurance provides in case of legal disputes?

Have I invested enough to keep me and my company safe in the event of any legal disputes?

Payroll Taxes

The federal government is quite stringent on payroll taxes. You can destroy your business if you do not pay them. Your accountant is your best asset in making sure your taxes are current. If you have employees, you will also benefit from hiring a payroll company to process these taxes before you hire your staff. I advise business owners it is better safe than sorry and not to take shortcuts here. If you are paying people under the table and not paying taxes, the government will show no mercy. Typically, the government will charge you with fines and penalties double, or even triple, what you should have paid. You will be required to pay all of it, and the government may shut down your business.

Forgetting about taxes. Do not operate without paying taxes. It will not end well. You may forget about taxes when you start your business, but Uncle Sam will not forget about you. Not figuring out what you owe and not paying taxes is one of the biggest mistakes business owners make. That is one of the fastest ways to kill your business. The government's regulations are in place to make it painful to violate them so you will not do it again.

Government-Regulated Labor Laws

Before you decide to hire employees, write (or pay someone else to write) a comprehensive employee manual. Once you start hiring, make sure every employee receives a copy and signs off on company policies.

Also develop a standard set of questions to ask potential employees and hiring guidelines, and put them in writing. This will protect you and your business if someone accuses you of discrimination.

Document everything, including why you did or did not hire each person who has gone through the interview process. Create a file for each person you interview (hard copy and digital), and keep those records handy. Attorneys love these types of cases because they are low-cost and many business owners settle out of court. Business owners' attorneys will often advise their clients to settle to keep the case out of court because judges and juries tend to favor plaintiff employees, not defendant business owners.

As a business owner, you become a target for false claims and suits because many people believe business owners have a lot of money. That is the perception. And even if they know you do not have money, they assume you have insurance that will pay out if you are taken to court.

If you would rather have a third party handle hiring practices for you, consider outsourcing to a human resource company specializing in reviewing candidates' qualifications. They can make decisions about who would be best for your company and send you several anonymous resumes for you to consider so you are choosing based on qualifications and not names or personal details.

Taking shortcuts. Take care of certain issues up front, such as employee manuals, insurance, an HR firm, and a good accountant. These tools serve as different layers of protection for you and your company. If you cannot afford them, perhaps you are not ready to be in business.

A BUSINESS OWNER'S BEST FRIEND

Throughout this book, I sing the praises of good accountants. Believe it or not, your accountant will become your best friend on your small-business journey. When I face many issues, I will reach out to my accountant before I call an attorney. After you have consulted with your accountant, he or she can then recommend a good lawyer for your particular situation. To find a good accountant, ask around. Check with your mentor, family members, friends, other business owners, and the Better Business Bureau. When you are reviewing accountants' resumes, look for whether they are in good standing with the CPA to make sure they do not have any violations against them.

CHAPTER 5

CREATING YOUR NETWORK OF SUPPORT

While there are some hurdles to becoming a business owner, you do not have to go it alone. You will find many individuals and organizations available to help you with virtually anything you will need, from sourcing funds to getting your paperwork in order to marketing your business. And some of the people who are ready to offer support may be closer to you than you think! I encourage business owners not to be too proud or afraid to seek support. There are executives who are willing to mentor and advise you. I think you will find your network of support may be one of the most valuable asset you have in building your business.

Seeking Support

You may not know it, but you are surrounded by potential mentors and advisors, many of them available for little to no cost to you. There is no shortage of executives who want to help the next generation of business owners to be successful. Where do you look for support?

Pastors and church clergy. Many pastors are involved in civic and community activities, they often have their fingers on the pulse of what is going on in your community, and they know the influential people who make it happen. Often, they own businesses, too, so they have a good network of people they might be willing to share with you. Start by asking your pastor or clergy, or talk with family members and friends who may be able to recommend their pastors.

SBA and SCORE. As with most things related to small businesses, the SBA/SCORE programs are an ideal resource for you as you seek mentors. They offer mentorships and counseling services, and they can recommend fellow business owners who have expertise in your field. Contact your local SBA office, or contact SBA online at sba.gov.

Local colleges and universities. Business professionals engage with professors and students through the schools' business programs. Some of the schools in your area may have business centers that will have mentor/counseling directories you can gain access to.

Business owners in your community. You probably come into contact with other business owners regularly. You see how their businesses are doing, and you admire their progress and growth. It may be as simple as approaching them and asking if they have time to talk with you about mentorship. Let them know you are trying to start or grow your business and could benefit from their expertise. Do not be too proud to ask for their help or afraid they will not help because you are just starting out. They can only say yes or no, but you will not know until you ask.

In searching for a mentor, you may find several people who fit your counseling needs. Is it okay to have more than one mentor? Absolutely! You can never have too much information. (Although I would caution you to develop discernment that will help you sort through what is valuable information and what is not.) Your perspective can be deeply enriched by talking with people who have different levels of experience.

Good mentors are transparent. They can tell you about the good old days, the bad old days, and how they coped with both. And while I am telling you about the good and the bad, do not feel you need to limit the scope of your mentor search to people who can help you with your business. Although you are becoming a business owner, you are still a person, with all that involves. Especially in the beginning, you may not be able to adequately separate your personal life from your business life, and you may need someone you can talk with about the dichotomy.

You may have a mentor to help you talk through your day, a mentor to help you with the numbers and analyze your financials, a mentor to help you with sales, and a mentor to help you with marketing. No one person knows everything, and you can benefit from the knowledge of many mentors on a variety of subjects.

Coaching

You have probably heard of certified life coaches and certified business coaches. Let me preface what I am going to say by giving you a disclaimer: I am not against certified

---

GIVING SUPPORT

As a SCORE counselor, I cannot recommend this program highly enough. You will reach a place in your business journey where you will want to give back in a meaningful way. Volunteering to mentor and coach the next generation of business owners is an excellent way to do that. Believe it or not, as you offer support to other small-business owners, you will still receive many positive benefits, too. You can develop new skills, gain exposure for your business, and expand your own network of support. If you are considering becoming a SCORE volunteer, go to score.org, and read their extensive volunteer resources.

coaches. In many ways, they are similar to mentors; and in some circumstances, they can help you get good results as you pursue business ownership.

Having said that, I caution you to do your homework and use discernment when paying for the services of a "certified" coach. First, check a coach's certification. If the certification is not accredited by a reputable body, then you should probably steer clear. There are recognized accreditation bodies that grant certificates to coaches. Check with the Better Business Bureau or trusted business professionals to see if the certifications are legitimate.

Second, although I have emphasized areas throughout this book where it is not a good idea to cut corners and not pay for something, this is not of them. There are too many mentorship resources available to you for you to pay someone to coach you, especially if you cannot be absolutely sure of their qualifications before you pay them. Trust me, that is the quickest way to buyer's remorse.

How do I know? I had an unpleasant experience years ago, and I hope by sharing it with you, you can avoid that pitfall.

I met a "business coach" through a networking group. He told me his fee was over a thousand dollars a month for his "services." I did not know any better, and I hired him. When I saw how little he brought to the table, and I discovered I knew much more about the matter than he did, I realized I had just wasted money.

Do not do as I did. Be wary of people who hand you business cards with "certified _____ coach" behind their names. Some of them are not certified; others are certified, but their certificate is not accredited and they do not have any real expertise. Instead, save your money, or invest it into other, worthier aspects of your business.

I PUT MY PRIDE ASIDE

I met a fellow business man here in Birmingham who is a little older than I am. We saw each other at different events; however, we were not friends. But I was observing him, and I noticed he was doing extremely well in business. I said to myself, *I need to just put my pride aside and talk with him about his success. How did he do it, and is there anything he can say that would help me?* I got up my courage and asked if I could talk with him. He said, "I'd be honored." We became fast friends, even outside of business; and when it is time to talk business, I know I can go to him.

Must-have Qualities for a Small-Business Mentor[1]

Top Ten Qualities of a Great Mentor	
1. Challenges You	A great mentor always pushes you to be better and never lets you rest on your laurels.
2. Has Experience	Your mentor should have a ton of relevant experience and wisdom they can draw upon.
3. Is Already Where You Want to Be	Choose a mentor that shares the same vision of success as you.
4. Supports You	A great mentor will pick you up when you stumble and fall.
5. Is a Great Listener	Your mentor should be willing to listen to more than just his or her own opinion.
6. Is Invested in Your Success	Great mentors are happy to see you succeed and even potentially surpass them.
7. Guides You Toward the Answer	Mentors should never just give you the answer, but give you the tools to figure it out yourself.
8. Provides Constructive Feedback	Your mentor will praise you when you've done right and, most important, help you figure out what went wrong.
9. Respects You	A great mentor should never look down on you but, instead, should see you as his or her equal.
10. Is Available	A great mentor should always be available to provide the help and advice you need.

 There are prominent business owners who willingly give of their time to mentor others, but there are some people you should steer clear of:

Anyone hiding a bad past. There are people who have a bad past and have come through the fire, so to speak, and they become mentors to help other people avoid the pitfalls they fell into. But they are transparent about their past up front. They are not trying to hide it and present themselves to you as someone they are not. When looking for a mentor, be wary of those who have bad marks in their background, unless they are transparent about it from the beginning.

Know-It-Alls. Even highly successful mentors do not know everything, so be cautious of those who pretend they do. Honest mentors tell you the limitations of their knowledge and do not mind connecting you with other people who can help you in areas where they do not have the expertise. You do not want someone offering theory when you need answers based in reality. For that, you need a mentor who has skin in the game. They have faced it, lived it, and survived it. If a mentor comes across as a know-it-all and is offended if you want to talk with other people, run!

Absentee Mentors. You are busy. You carve out time in your schedule to meet with your mentor, but he or she does not show up or cancels frequently. Perhaps your mentor is too busy right now, or he or she is going through a difficult time. Think carefully about what you need in a mentor, and if he or she is not offering it, find a respectful way to end the mentorship. (Of course, this works both ways. See "How to Be a Good Mentee" below.)

Be a Good Mentee

Now that I have shared with you what to look for in a mentor, I'd like to help you be a good mentee. You will meet many business executives who are willing to pour into you because they see your potential and they want to see you get to the next level. But if you are uncooperative, all of their time and energy will be completely wasted. Put in the work to be the best mentee you can be so you can benefit from the wealth of knowledge, skill, talent, resources, and information your mentors have to offer.

Be committed to your business. If you are treating your business like a hobby, a fly-by-night operation, you probably will not get very far. Mentors want to see you are all in and you are committed for the long-term. That makes sense, right? Why should they waste time with someone who will not be in business until the end of the year? If you need to take a break, let your mentor know. He or she will appreciate and respect your honesty and openness.

Listen. I know that can be difficult to do. You have a million and one things on your mind, and you can barely sit still as your mentor shares his or her experiences with you. Your phone keeps ringing, and you cannot remember what your mentor just said. That is not good. When you are with your mentor, be intentional about quieting your mind, silencing your phone, and leaning in to listen and hear what he or she has to say. Give the person your full attention.

Do not be combative. If you do not agree with something your mentor is saying, that is fine, but find a productive and respectful way to say it. I have had mentees argue with me about something I said, only to be proven wrong later. Mentors and mentees are entitled to their own opinions, but respect your mentor enough to agree to disagree instead of starting a fight or talking just to hear yourself talk. Value and respect your mentor's years of experience in the field. It could be he or she really does know more than you do.

Take action. A good mentor will carefully prepare his or her advice for you. He or she will have thought out what they are advising you to do based on experience and past successes or failures. It is disheartening and frustrating when a mentor sees mentees are completely ignoring the advice or doing the opposite.

I have mentored people who make no progress whatsoever on the action items we discuss. After several weeks, I know I have wasted my time with them. Take action on the things you discuss with your mentor. If you are struggling with something or do not understand it, bring it to the next session and discuss it. If the actions are not working, discuss that, too. Your mentor will be more than willing to adjust accordingly.

Be patient. The journey of business ownership is often long and winding, and progress can be slow at times. Your mentor knows this and is trying to help you through those times. He or she is trying to help you put long-term solutions in place. Be patient. You may not see immediate results after every session. Sales may not skyrocket like you want them to, and profits may not explode. Some of the things happening to you along the way cannot be foreseen, and you have to slow down and deal with things that might not have been in your business plan. But stay on track, and stay in touch with your mentor.

Be willing to walk away. Some mentors are not very good at what they do, or they can be toxic. If that is the case, respectfully—but quickly—find your way out of the mentorship. Perhaps there is nothing wrong with the mentor and you are doing everything you can, but it is just not a good fit. You can still respectfully walk away and find someone else. Be honest with your mentor instead of just walking away. You may be able to find someone more suitable after talking with your current mentor.

When I mentor up-and-coming business owners, I am looking for progress and growth. When my mentees text me or call me and excitedly tell me our sessions are helping and they are seeing the fruits of their labor, I know we've been successful.

ASK YOURSELF

Am I a good mentee? Is there room for improvement?

Is my relationship with my mentor productive or toxic?

If the relationship is toxic, how should I terminate the mentorship?

Have I made my action items a priority? If not, how can I do better?

Am I as committed to my business as I need to be?

Am I a good listener? If not, how can I improve?

CHAPTER 6

BUILDING YOUR BRAND

When you introduce yourself to other people, you are probably aware that impressions matter, especially first impressions. As a new business owner who wants to sell a product or a service, you will need to introduce yourself to the market. How you navigate it may make the difference between success and failure. There are some essential things you will need to know about the most effective ways to build your brand, perfect your messaging, and market your business. I mentor new business owners who believe all they need is a good social media approach. But having a successful presence in the market is so much more. Let us walk through some of the things you will need to know.

Identifying and Developing Your Brand

Before you can introduce yourself to anyone else, it helps to know who you are. Before you can introduce your business to the marketplace, find out what your business is. Do not allow your business to have an identity crisis by trying to be all things to all people. Spend time figuring out what you want your customers to know about your business, being as specific as possible.

Start with aesthetics. Often, customers make decisions on first impressions. Most of us do the same thing when we meet other people or sit down to eat at a restaurant. If our first impression of someone is not good, we probably will not befriend them. If the plate arrives at our table and has a hair on it, it will not matter how good the food might taste, we probably will not eat it.

No matter how good your product or service is, if you fail the first impressions test with enough customers, you probably will not be in business for long. If your website looks as if it was designed in the 1990s and is hard to navigate, customers are probably going to go elsewhere, and you will lose sales. If your business card is flimsy and the ink on it is smudged, potential customers probably are not going to call you and will throw it away at the soonest possibility.

This is the point, right from the beginning, when you up your game and pay the money necessary to start developing your brand. Once you have figured out exactly what your company is, you can start working on the aesthetics of your brand. Make sure everything associated with your company looks aboveboard so you can battle with your best competitor and blow your lowest competitor out of the water. Whether you do the work yourself or hire a professional, make sure everything from your website to your business cards to your brick-and-mortar store look as good as possible.

Start the habit of putting any written or digital correspondence on letterhead. It does not matter what your product or service is. Whether you are a plumber, gardener, HVAC technician, dress shop owner, pet store owner, or luxury real estate agent, your company's advertisements, brochures, and catalogs should not look as if you printed them off your home computer and you asked your children to help you fold and label them. Make sure your company's materials look professional, which gives more legitimacy to your business.

BRANDING MATTERS

According to Workhorse Marketing, "every aspect of your company says something about who you are and what you have to offer. Branding is important for every company to set itself apart from the competition and define its mission for both customers and employees."[1] Here are the top five reasons branding is important:

- Forms a strong customer bond
- Creates employee advocates
- Supports marketing and advertising efforts
- Drives a higher price point
- Builds a loyal customer base

Do as I Do, Not as I Did

ASK
YOURSELF

What is my business about?

How do I want potential customers to see my business?

How do I want to present my business to the marketplace?

How can my brand set my business apart from the competition?

Does my brand present a coherent message to my employees as well as to my customers? Why or why not?

Not investing the appropriate amount of resources. Many business owners fail to invest in their marketing because they do not know that they need to do so. That is why a marketing strategy is crucial to successfully building your brand.

Being Consistent

One of the fastest ways to tarnish your brand is to be haphazard with customers. Customers may be fickle, but they will expect *you* to be consistent and dependable. And if you

---

GETTING HELP

I mentor a woman who owns a food truck. She told me it was almost impossible for her to keep up her social media presence, which her business is heavily dependent on. Because she is mobile and stops in various locations around the city, she needs to stay in contact with her customers so they know where to find her or to tell them about new menu items. She was extremely frustrated, almost to the point of tears, because building and maintaining her brand had become overwhelming, and she found it difficult to keep up. Because she spends most of her days cooking, she just did not have time in the evenings to catch up. She found she could not be consistent.

She would be a perfect candidate for a branding company. Just as with most things, you can hire someone to provide branding services for you, which will more than likely include social media advertising and engagement. They will keep your customers updated on sales, new products or services, promo codes, and special events. If you find you are too busy to properly promote your brand, consider paying for a branding service to do it for you.

are consistent, you might find those fickle customers will become part of a loyal customer base.

I tell new business owners 80 percent of the battle is consistency. Is my building management company the best in the industry? Honestly, no. But over the years, we have been dedicated and consistent, and that is a major part of our brand. If a customer calls us, we answer the phone every time. Some of our customers have complained when they have had to call our competitors multiple times to speak with someone or they never got an answer; and there was absolutely no follow-up.

WHAT IS THE DIFFERENCE?

To the average person, the words *branding, messaging,* and *marketing* may mean the same thing; but they do not. And to be more savvy in presenting yourself effectively in the marketplace, it is important to know the difference.

Branding is the ultimate goal. It puts a laser focus on what your company is all about. For example, McDonald's is known all over the world for their hamburgers. They may sell other things, but hamburgers are their main focus. When you are branding your business, you are branding it with the primary thing you do best.

When you are consistent, customers get to know your company. They can trust you will be there, someone will pick up the phone, and you will keep your promises. If you outsource the elements of your business your customers have come to rely on, you may not be able to keep them for long. There is nothing wrong with outsourcing when you have to. In the beginning, it may be what you have to do on a limited budget. But work as hard as you can to make it a priority to pull those aspects back in so you can be there for your customers.

Messaging involves the components of what you want to try to identify within the brand. For example, Gatorade used Michael Jordan as a tool to expose their drink as the best one in the world. They combined the best drink with the best basketball player so customers would make the association in their minds and buy their drink.

Marketing is the arm that moves your brand. How do you get your message out to the masses? What does that look like? You can use networking, advertising, flash sale marketing, to name a few. Those are a few of the avenues through which you can expose your brand to the public, and the more marketing you do, the bigger your audience can be. It can go from local to global.

ASK YOURSELF

Is my business consistent with my customers? If so, how? If not, why not?

If I am not consistent, how can I improve?

What can I do to show customers I am committed to serving them and I can do that better than my competitors?

Develop a Marketing Strategy

Speaking of costs, having a marketing strategy will help you to think through some of the financial decisions you will need to make. You will need to ask yourself, *What can I do for free versus what do I need to do to pay for it?* Sometimes those decisions can be made in phases. A marketing strategy is especially helpful when you work with a team of people.

In the beginning, you may not be able to afford many of the services you need. If that is the case, visit your local chamber of commerce. They usually maintain a comprehensive list of services and providers, which can be a great resource for small businesses with small budgets. The chamber of commerce also hosts networking events, which can be one of the most effective tools to get your brand into the marketplace after you have done your initial work.

Unfortunately, some business owners do not have a marketing strategy, and they often hire the wrong people to help them develop their brand. They believe their success will develop organically, but this is where a marketing strategy comes in handy. By specifying your needs in great detail in your marketing strategy, you can make everyone aware of how you need them to move as it relates to your brand, and you can keep everyone on the same page.

If I'm on a small budget, what can I do at no cost, or low cost, to develop my brand and market my business?

What do I need to include in my marketing strategy that will keep all of my team members on the same page as far as my business needs?

How much am I wiling to invest in the beginning to ensure my business is successful?

Hiring the wrong people to help you build and market your brand. In any industry, there are dishonest and incapable people who will talk you into hiring them to work on your brand. They do this by feeding off of your needs or your fear. But they do not know about your business, neither do they understand what you really need. If you do not understand how to use marketing tools, others will take advantage of you.

Assuming building your brand is easy. Some business owners assume they can easily figure out the marketing aspect of their business and it will just happen. They do not necessarily respect the discipline and how the market moves through research and artistic and analytical data.

Establishing your business marketing only on what feels good. Some business owners rely on their personal feelings or their emotions. But marketing is a discipline and should be treated as such. If you are not sure how to approach it, then a trusted professional can help.

Social Media

Believe it or not, social media is not the end-all be-all of marketing. While it can be an effective tool, it depends on how you use it. It is not by any means a one-size-fits-all solution. Many people assume celebrities and other popular social media influencers can effectively sell merchandise because they have huge followings. But a social media presence does not always translate to sales.

If you do not know how to successfully navigate social media and how to use it to promote your brand, you will miss out on what it can actually be used for. No matter how many expensive tools you own, if you do not know how to use them, they are of no value to you. Social media is a good tool, but if you do not know how to use it for your particular business, you will not get any value out of it.

Networking

Many business owners miss out on a golden opportunity to build their brand and let people know about their businesses. They may assume they need to spend far more money when they could attend networking events that could put them in the company of people who can help carry the message about their business.

According to Ann Evanston, an entrepreneurial consultant, there are several ways business owners can use networking to market their businesses:

Be prepared for every networking event. Do not expect things to "just happen" once you arrive. Have a plan before you go.

Do not go to networking events just to sell. There are other benefits to be found and, in the process, you may connect with people who can help you sell your product by word of mouth.

Be a great listener and a giver. It may sound counterintuitive, but when you realize the benefits of attending networking events, you will understand why engaging with others is crucial.

Follow up. This is key. It can make or break future connections.[2]

ASK YOURSELF

How have I used social media thus far to build my brand and announce my presence in the marketplace?

What have I assumed about social media engagement that may have harmed my marketing efforts?

CHAPTER 7

ATTRACTING AND KEEPING CUSTOMERS

Without customers, your business is just a hobby, and you are not taking risks and putting everything on the line for a hobby! You will need to attract people to your business who believe you can provide them with the products and services they need and want. And you will want to keep them coming back again and again because you offer a quality product or service and excellent customer care. If you successfully build your brand and effectively make your presence known in the market (see Chapter 6), you will not have problems attracting customers. But I want to help you know how to keep them, even when you have stiff competition from larger companies offering more than you do.

Attracting Customers

All of your paperwork is in order, you have received funding, built your brand, and hired employees. Now you are ready to throw open your (real or virtual) doors. How do you attract customers?

Start close to home. Your family members and closest friends could possibly be your first customers. Talk with them and see if they will support you. Because of your established relationships, you are more likely to get their interest, and they can also spread the word of your services.

Think about people you worked with in the past or former clients. When I started my business, I contacted some of the clients I had from my days working in banking. I found those were softer sales, and I had a greater chance of gaining them as clients than from cold calls and strangers. Consider reconnecting with people you worked with in the past. You might find they are willing to support you.

Cast your net wide. Some of your customers may come from unexpected places. They will not all come from your community or even from your social media followers. Be open-minded to attracting customers through various avenues. I have never believed I could get all of my customers from one source. I like to keep open as many doors as possible: social media, networking, radio, and telemarketing.

But keep an eye on your budget when casting your net. If there is an avenue you are using that is not giving you enough of a dividend and you cannot justify the expense, consider terminating it and using the money elsewhere. Radio spots are quite expensive, so if I see I am not getting enough foot traffic based on my radio spots, then I am going to discontinue advertising there. Then I am going to look for other aspects of my business in which I can invest the money.

I used to be a member of the chamber of commerce. I had heard it was difficult to make business connections there, but I thought I'd try. After a year, I hadn't gotten much out of my membership, not even a warm lead. I decided to cancel my membership and put my money elsewhere. But when you are looking at your budget and analyzing what is working or not working for you, think about more than just the money. You also need to consider the time, effort, and energy you are putting into a particular avenue to attract customers with no return.

Do as I Do, Not as I Did

ASK YOURSELF

How wide have I cast my net?

What avenues have I used to attract potential customers?

Are there avenues that are not working for me right now? What other avenues are open to me?

Research the Competition

You are not operating your business in a vacuum, and you are probably not the only game in town. You will need to be aware of your competition and find out more about it so you can successfully attract customers to your business.

How do you research your competition?

Ask your current clients what they like and do not like. Find out what their pain points are as it relates to the type of product or service you are offering.

Do an internet search for your competition. Look at their websites. See if their marketing materials are up to industry standards. See if they offer anything extra you have not thought to offer. Consider offering something they do not.

Visit different local businesses. If it makes sense to do so, visit your local competition. Observe their operations for yourself, and experience their customer service. See how your business practices may differ.

My company is able to do everything in the building services and commercial janitorial industry. But there are a lot of companies that do not have the capabilities to do what my company can do. They also do not have the type of insurance binders that allow them to offer some of the services my company has. I can attract the larger clients because they require certain insurance coverages and training smaller businesses cannot afford, but we can. Your research can help you to position your company to attract the best customers, even with stiff competition.

ASK YOURSELF

Who is my competition?

What are they offering that I am not offering?

What am I offering that they do not offer?

Have I talked with my customers? What are they saying about pain points and what my competition is offering?

Keeping Customers

Customers can be fickle and not loyal at all. If they do not like the products or services you offer, they will vote with their wallets and with their feet. They will usually go where they feel they are getting a better deal and better customer care. But if they find a company that caters to them and provides what they want and need, they will be loyal. You want to do everything you can to attract *and* keep your customers. There are quite easy steps to make sure that happens.

Keep your promises. If you tell your customers you are going to do something or provide an extra service, keep your promises. As the saying goes, "Under-promise, and over-deliver." I tell my clients my staff is only human. Sometimes we make mistakes. For me, it is not that we make mistakes, but how we react when we discover we have made them. That is when we show our integrity and ethics. I teach my staff we should acknowledge the mistakes and make them right.

Stay in contact. The supervisors at my company meet with our clients biweekly. If that does not suit our clients' needs, we can adjust our follow-up accordingly. And when we meet with our customers, we listen intently to what they want. Customers value that type of engagement. And by staying in contact, you can stay in front of any problems, and you will find you can better anticipate your clients' needs.

Ask your current customers for referrals. Your customers will usually be flattered you trust them enough to ask them to send their friends to you. And that is a good way to build a solid relationship with your current and future customers.

Never get comfortable or complacent. In my business, I never rest on our current status and assume it will be the same a year, five years, ten years from now. I advise you not to get too comfortable either. Your competition is always hungry and looking for a piece of your business.

Consider customer loyalty programs. These can be a good incentive to keep your clients satisfied and wanting to return. I know of a company that treats their big-dollar clients to hunting trips. If their clients spend more than a quarter of a million dollars with them in a fiscal year, those clients can take part in the trips. You may not be able to offer such an expensive incentive. But you can reward them with small discounts and bonuses. If they pay their invoices early, you could give them a two-percent discount, or you could send them small thank-you gifts.

What is my strategy for keeping my customers?

Have I ever gotten complacent about my customer base? If so, what happened?

If I could afford some type of customer loyalty program or incentive program, what would it look like?

If my budget is small, what can I offer my customers?

Customer Service[1]

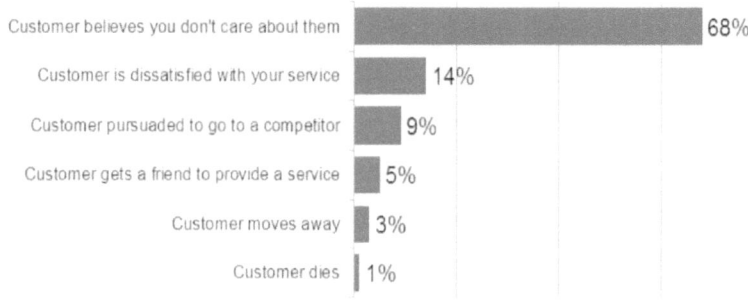

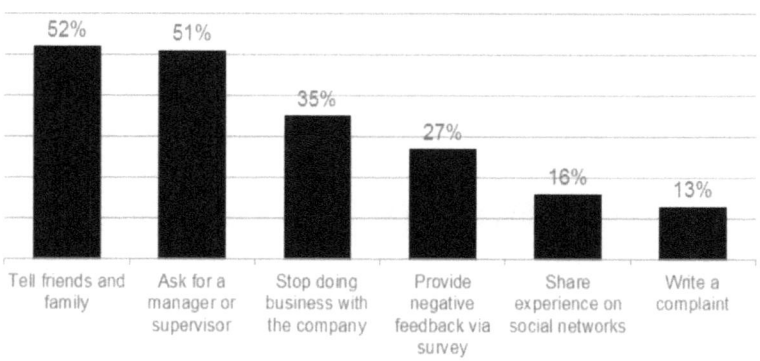

Create Stellar Customer Care

Some companies seem nonchalant about customer service. They do not return phone calls, they do not follow up, and they do not respond to customers' concerns or needs. For my business, customer service is a priority.

If our clients need something, we drop whatever we are doing to attend to it. If they email us, we do not make them wait 24 hours. We respond immediately. An essential part of training at my company involves everyone in customer care, from the front line to the back end. And my staff is trained to look for ways to delight our customers, even if it requires giving them something extra.

People like to feel appreciated, and our customer care helps them to feel they are important to us. If you create customer loyalty, your customers will not feel they can go anywhere else and receive the stellar customer care you offer.

On the rare occasion we have an unhappy customer, we do not get upset about it. Instead, we see it as a good thing, and we use it as a learning opportunity. We appreciate unhappy customers who voice their displeasure with us. Unhappy customers who do not let us know what went wrong but simply walk away and never return do not help us. But with our vocal customers—especially the unhappy ones—we have an opportunity to get it right. We take our customer care seriously because our customers drive our business.

Customer Service[2]

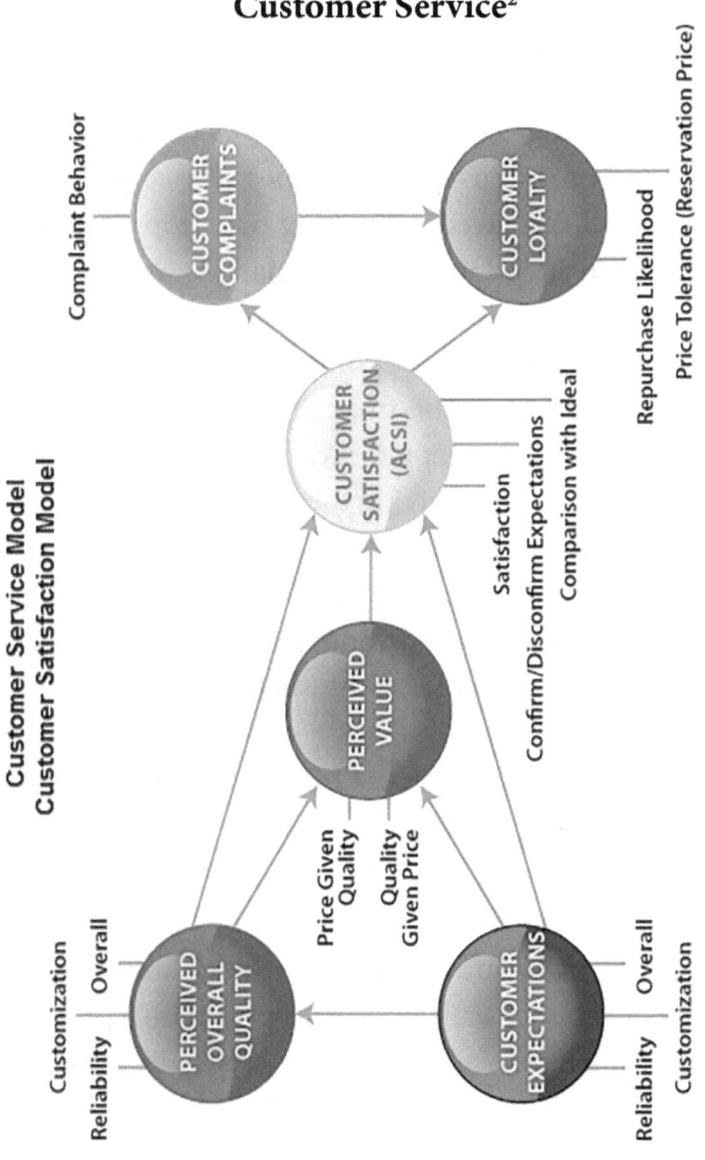

ASK YOURSELF

What is my idea of stellar customer care?

What do I do when I encounter unhappy customers?

How do I correct mistakes and make things right?

Putting the wrong people in the wrong positions. When you first start out, you are grateful to almost anyone who helps and supports you. But sometimes those who seem eager to help can hurt your business, especially if they have to deal with your customers. I admit it. I have made the mistake of hiring family members. They said they needed a job, and I am a nice guy. I just wanted to help them, and I sure needed the help. But I learned the hard way you have to hire the right kind of people for the right kind of job. There is nothing wrong with helping out family members and friends, but be careful when you hire them. They probably do not have the interest or investment in your business you do. For them, the job you give them is a means to a paycheck—nothing more, nothing less. If they have a bad attitude, give terrible customer service, or cannot handle unhappy customers, then it is probably not a good idea to hire them or keep them on the job.

CHAPTER 8

GROWING YOUR BUSINESS

Y ou may be starting your business as a side job you do on weekends while you work a regular job, but one of your main goals should be to eventually grow and expand your business. That might look different for different people, depending on the type of business they have. But I want to encourage you that growing and expanding your business is possible, and I advise you not to wait until the distant future to plan for growth. The best time to think about growth is when you first get started so you can successfully map out your plans and make good decisions now. Fortunately, you can turn to your network of support to help you to plan for the future. And in this chapter, you can explore different ways to help you make those plans a reality.

Now That You Are Ready to Grow . . .

I encourage new business owners to start planning for growth from day one. It is never too early. Having said that, be patient. Growth does not happen overnight. It will take time, and you will need to put in some hard work. You will need to keep your head down and focus exclusively on your work, but you cannot do that always and still focus on growing your business. At some point, you will need to take the leap and begin the incremental steps to growth. If you do not, you may become stagnant or, worse, lose ground.

I talked to another business owner about growing his business. He told me how busy he is, and he asked me when would be a good time to bring on staff. But then he confided in me he was afraid to hire anyone because he preferred to do everything himself. He was afraid if he hired employees, they might mess up, and he did not want to take money out of his pocket for payroll to pay people to mess up.

I told him we are all human and have the capacity to make mistakes. As an employer, he should expect a certain level of "mess-up-ability." But it is a trade-off. If he hired staff, it would free him up to do other things. The money he would pay in salaries would be worth it to him in the long run. That is just all part of running a business.

Once you start to grow your business, you can see how you can expand in increments because you are not so preoccupied with the minutiae of running your business. You can also justify the increase in staff and spending because you need more people to absorb the responsibilities of your growing business. In time, you will see the extra costs begin to pay for themselves. I'd rather bring on extra staff and pay them good salaries than to see my employees get burned out because they are taking on too much. Thus, the quality of the service we provide would deteriorate.

GROWTH DOES NOT HAVE TO BE SHOWY

I knew someone who had a landscaping company. One day, he bought a $50,000 truck for his business. When I asked him why, he said he wanted a nice truck to put his name on to advertise the company. I thought that was mistake. The old truck he had was just fine. He was hauling around dirty lawnmowers and weed-eaters. A brand-new truck may be fine for a high-level business, but what good does it do to drive an expensive truck when your company has a downturn or the growth stalls? He could have taken the same money and invested it in marketing and advertising to get more customers, to get better and more efficient equipment, or to raise his employees' salaries.

ASK YOURSELF

When did I first start planning for my company's growth?

What are my criteria for growth?

How do I know I am ready for growth?

Am I willing to take incremental steps, or am I impatient to expand?

Handle Your Money Responsibly as You Grow

As your business grows, obviously, you will see increased revenue. But do not be tempted to spend your earnings, even if you feel you deserve to as a way of rewarding yourself for your success. Wise entrepreneurs will save a portion of those earnings for a rainy day and invest the rest back into the company. There are probably many areas of your business you can improve and upgrade, which will put you in an even better position for growth.

A growth plan should already be part of your business plan. If it is not, now is the time to add it. Your growth plan will outline how much you should set aside regularly, which will help you prepare for any adverse situation that may arise. As I have said before, you want to always be ready for the bigger clients to come your way, and they will not wait for several weeks while you try to raise the money you need.

Buying things you do not need. Although you are ready for growth, be careful how you spend your money. Think about the equipment and other inventory you will need, and spend wisely. Do not just buy things because you can. Create a budget, and stick to it. Do not be afraid to take incremental steps to growth, but do not rush and try to expand too soon.

ASK YOURSELF

How do I think my budget will change once my company grows?

Does my growth plan include financial forecasts? If so, what does that look like?

How disciplined would I be in spending and investing my company's increased revenue?

Ways to Grow Your Business on a Budget

You might think you have to wait until you have increased sales and revenue before you can begin to grow. But as you know, I encourage you to think growth from the time you establish your business. How can you plan for that when you are starting out and have a reduced budget and resources?

According to marketing and advertising professionals Ken Burgin and Elizabeth Walker, there are many ways you can begin to grow your business with little to no money. Read through the list and see which ways you might be able to implement now, and consider adding them to your growth plan.[1]

Bill faster. Instead of batch invoicing, bill as soon as you can.

Streamline your business. My scalable business is streamlined and flexible. If I have to, I can move from one city to another with no problem. I do not buy what I do not need, and if something I have is not working, I get rid of it.

Increase your visibility. Learn about search engine optimization so your business will more likely show up on the first page of a potential customer's search results.

Delegate. Focus more on what makes money, and delegate the rest to someone else.

Work faster. This could also be part of simplifying and streamlining your business. The faster you work, the more work you can do, and the more money you will make.

Promote your business consistently. Make sure customers have the most current information about your business, especially if you do not have a brick-and-mortar building. Make them aware of promotions, sales, and events to give them every opportunity to stay loyal members of your customer base.

Encourage your supporters to refer you. This is part of casting your net wide and not rejecting any avenue to promote your business.

Steps to Growth

Do not feel you have to take all of the steps at once. Read through them, and consider which steps make sense for you in your present phase of business ownership. Other steps you will need to revisit in the future when you have experienced more growth. But for now, you can include many of these steps in your business plan under your strategies for expansion.

Keep and grow your customer base. When you have long-standing customers, you are more confident of getting regular revenue. When you have a regular revenue stream, you can more confidently make plans and put money aside for further growth.

Make your business as scalable as possible. The reason I went into the janitorial and building management industry is because it is easily scalable. I can duplicate what I do almost anywhere I go, which makes it simple to establish systems and processes. That may make my business seem very cookie-cutter, which, in a way, it is. But it makes it easy for me to pick up everything and move to another location. I have been able to keep my business fluid and flexible. I can adjust whenever I need to and meet varied needs when other companies cannot do so.

Consider acquiring another business. I am always on the lookout for companies I might buy. If I acquire another business, the purchase would immediately expand because I would be able to integrate it into my current company. A good way to acquire another company is to look for a business owner who wants to retire, is tired of the business, or has taken on more than he or she wants to take care of.

Consider a merger. You might be doing well with your business, or maybe you are feeling somewhat overwhelmed. Then you may meet another business owner who is experiencing the same thing. Together, you might discuss how your companies would be better if you merged your efforts or pursued a joint venture. If you merge with another company, you would form one company legally, but each person would control 50 percent. You would also gain a larger clientele you probably would not be able to attract on your own. Your newly acquired and larger clientele would bring in bigger revenue, which you could put toward those big-dollar projects.

ASK YOURSELF

After reading through the steps for growth, which steps would be appropriate for me to take now or in the immediate future?

What steps would I rather follow in later phases of my entrepreneurial journey?

Additional Resources

SCORE has a comprehensive library of digital resources that can help you on your entrepreneurial journey. There are helpful webinars, articles, and videos. Here is a short list of relevant resources related to some of the material found in this book. For more information, visit SCORE's website at score.org.

- "Determining Your Company's Legal Structure" (course on demand)
- "Customer Service: Small Business, Big Advantage" (eGuide)
- "How to Get Certified as a Minority-Owned Business" (blog)
- "The Startup Roadmap" (course on demand)
- "Funding Options for Veteran Entrepreneurs" (recorded webinar)
- "Strategically and Successfully Grow Your Small Business" (recorded webinar)

Sources

Chapter 2
[1] Based on "7 Popular Business Structures," Corpnet.com (corpnet.com/start-business/business-structures-chart/).

[2] "Right of First Offer vs. Right of First Refusal," by Pat Kelley, SmallBusiness.Chronicle.com (January 31, 2019).

Chapter 3
[1] Based on "How to Finance a Business: Everything You Need to Know," "Best Small Business Financing Options: A Quick Comparison" chart, by Meredith Wood, Fundera (October 2, 2020).

Chapter 4
[1] "Workers' Compensation Insurance vs. General Liability: What's the Difference?" WorkCompOne (workcompone.com/blog/general-liability-workers-compensation).

Chapter 5
[1] "8 Must-have Qualities for a Small Business Mentor," The Brand Boy Small Business Blog (thebrandboy.com/qualities-for-business-mentor/).

Chapter 6
[1] "5 Reasons Why Great Branding Matters," by Guy Parker, Workhorse Marketing, May 3, 2018 (workhorsemktcom/5-reasons-branding-matters/).

[2] "4 Ways to Successful Networking as a Marketing Strategy," by Ann Evanston, Small Business Marketing Tools (sbmarketingtools.com/4-ways-successful-networking-marketing-strategy/).

Chapter 7
[1] "What Is the Purpose of Help Desk in a Business?" (Sourced from The Rockefeller Corporation and ClickFox), FinancesOnline.

[2] Based on "Customer Service Model, Customer Satisfaction Model," available through Creative Commons (ygraph.com/chart/2644) (creativecommons.org/licenses/by/3.0/).